TUNE

IN▪▪

to the **VOICE** of **GOD**

KENNETH
COPELAND
PUBLICATIONS

Unless otherwise noted, all scripture is from the *King James Version* of the Bible.

Scripture quotations marked *The Amplified Bible* are from *The Amplified Bible, Old Testament* © 1965, 1987 by the Zondervan Corporation. *The Amplified New Testament* © 1958, 1987 by The Lockman Foundation. Used by permission.

Scripture quotations marked *New King James Version* are from the *New King James Version* © 1982 by Thomas Nelson Inc.

Tune In to the Voice of God

ISBN 978-1-60463-108-1   30-0071

16 15 14 13 12 11   6 5 4 3 2 1

© 2004 Eagle Mountain International Church Inc. aka Kenneth Copeland Ministries

Kenneth Copeland Publications
Fort Worth, TX 76192-0001

For more information about Kenneth Copeland Ministries, call 800-600-7395 or visit www.kcm.org.

Tune In to the Voice of God

What is the Spirit of God saying to you today? What is He telling you about your spiritual development… your family…and your finances? If you're facing trouble, what word of victory has He spoken to you?

As a born-again child of the living God, you ought to know the answers to those questions.

I've learned by experience, however, the majority of believers don't. I can tell by just listening to them talk. "Oh, my goodness," they'll say, "I'm in a crisis and I don't know what to do!"

If that's your situation, I'm going to be straight with you. You'd better go to God and find out what to do. You'd better be quiet long enough to hear what He has to say and pay attention to it. You'd better get rid of that fear and start believing God. Otherwise, the devil is going to end up getting the best of you.

If you read the Bible you'll see God has been trying to get His people to understand that for thousands of years. In fact, He gave those exact instructions to an Old Testament king named Ahaz back in the days of the prophet Isaiah. Ahaz was in serious trouble at the time. He had two enemy armies coming against him and he had no idea what to do about it. So God sent His Word to Ahaz through the prophet Isaiah and gave him a whole new perspective.

Instead of agreeing with Ahaz about how powerful his enemies were, God let him know they didn't impress Him much. He referred to them as two "smoking stumps" (Isaiah 7:4, *The Amplified Bible*). Then He assured Ahaz their plans against him would not stand if he would simply obey the following instructions: *Take heed...be quiet...fear not* (verse 4)...and *believe* (verse 9).

Check Your Receiver

Before you head down the road looking for a prophet like Isaiah to tell you what God is saying to you, let me save you a trip. You don't need a prophet to tell you what to do. You have a better covenant than Ahaz had. You're not just a servant of God like people were in the Old Covenant. Through the blood of Jesus, you've become a full-fledged son and the Bible says, "For as many as are led by the Spirit of God, they are the sons of God" (Romans 8:14).

Jesus confirmed that fact in John 10 when He said that His "sheep hear his voice; and he calls his own sheep by name and leads them out. And when he brings out his own sheep, he goes before them; and the sheep follow him, for they know his voice" (verses 3-4, *New King James Version).*

As a child of Almighty God, you have the right and the spiritual ability to hear the voice of God for yourself!

"But, Brother Copeland," you might say, "God never speaks to me."

Sure He does. You're just not listening.

Have you ever turned on your television and found something was wrong with the picture? Maybe it was fuzzy or the sound was crackling with static. Or maybe you couldn't get a picture at all. Did you grab the telephone, call NBC and tell them that something was wrong with their transmitter? Did you get some television executive on the line and say, "Hey, you guys must not be broadcasting anymore. I turned on my set and you weren't there!"

Certainly not! That didn't even occur to you. You were smart enough

7

to figure out the problem most likely wasn't with the transmitter. The problem was with the receiver. The problem was with your own television set.

So instead of blaming the broadcaster, you started trying to find the problem on your end. You might have checked the electrical connections. You might have looked to make sure the cable was hooked up. You might have checked the settings on the television to make sure they were all adjusted correctly.

What's more, you stayed with it until you got it fixed. Why? Because you never doubted the fact that the networks were still broadcasting. You understood if you could just successfully tune in, they would be there for you.

Find His Frequency

Don't you think we ought to have at least as much faith in God as we have in the television networks? They can break down. They can fail us. But God never will. He has given us His Word. He has promised He'll lead us by His Spirit and enable us to know His voice. So if we're having difficulty with those things, we need to stop blaming Him and determine where we're missing it.

Actually, that's not hard to do. When we have trouble hearing God's voice, it's almost always for one of the following four reasons:

- We don't believe He is speaking.

- We're not paying attention.

- We're allowing some kind of interference to drown out His voice.

- We just plain don't know what frequency He is on.

Let's focus right now on that last point. Exactly how do you locate the frequency God uses to speak to you?

I'll tell you right off the bat, you don't do it by using those fleshly paddles on the sides of your head—your natural ears. Some people try to hear God that way. They think if He would just speak audibly to them everything would be solved.

They're mistaken. Our natural ears weren't designed to hear the voice of God.

We were created to hear Him in our inner man or what the New Testament calls "the hidden man of the heart" (1 Peter 3:4).

As Hebrews 3:7-8 says, "Wherefore (as the Holy Ghost saith, Today if ye will hear his voice, harden not your hearts...)."

God leads His children not by outward voices or signs and wonders but by the inward witness of "the hidden man of the heart." So to find His frequency, the first thing you'll have to do is tune in—*not with your head but with your heart!*

Learn to Discern

How do you know the difference

between your head and your heart?

Scripturally speaking, your head is your soul, which is comprised of your mind, will and emotions. Your heart is your spirit, which is the core of your being that has been born again and joined to the Spirit of God. Granted, discerning the difference between the voice of your soul and the voice of your spirit can be challenging, and it takes spiritual wisdom to do it. But the Bible tells us clearly how to develop that wisdom: *We do it by spending time in the written Word of God.*

Hebrews 4:12 tells us that The Word is "quick, and powerful, and sharper than any twoedged sword, piercing even to the dividing asunder of soul and spirit, and of the joints and marrow, and is a discerner of the thoughts and intents of the heart." It contains the voice of God in its most tangible form.

God always agrees with His written Word and His Word always agrees with Him. In fact, Psalm 138:2 says He has magnified His Word even above His Name. That means God has put His Name on His written Word the way we would put our name at the bottom of a contract. He has given us His Word as a covenant and signed it in the Name of Jesus by the blood of Jesus.

Since God cannot lie, there is no way He will ever do or say anything contrary to that Word. He has absolutely joined Himself to it forever. So the first place God takes us to train us to recognize His voice is to His written Word. He uses it to tune our spiritual ears to the real so that we can easily recognize a counterfeit.

Have you ever watched an impersonator mimic a celebrity? If he is good at what he does, you'll think, *I know who that guy is impersonating. It's so-and-so. He sounds just like him!* But if you were to put the real personality right next to the impersonator, the differences would be glaring. If you could see them both at the same time, you'd think, *That guy doesn't sound much like him at all!*

That's the way it is with God's written Word. The better you know it, the more you've heard God's voice speaking to you through it, the easier it is for you to tell the difference between His voice and another voice. The easier it is for you to divide your soul from your spirit and discern the difference between the voice of your head and the voice of your heart.

When you're trained to hear God's voice in His Word, the devil won't be able to sneak deceptions in on you, either. When he tries to razzle-dazzle you with some religious-sounding voice that says, *I love you, my son. But it's just not my will to heal you at this time,* you won't buy it. You'll rise up and say, "That's not the voice of God. That's a lie from hell because it doesn't agree with The Word that says 'by His stripes ye were healed.'"

Let me warn you though, you won't get that kind of training just casually reading the Bible now and then. You won't get it by knowing generally what it says…or by mixing what it says with your own opinions. If you desire to truly learn to hear the voice of God in The Word, you'll have to do with it what God told Ahaz to do.

You'll have to take heed to it. You'll have to pay attention!

Zero In

Paying attention is more than just mentally assenting to a scripture and saying, "Oh yes, hallelujah. Amen." To pay attention means to lock in on what's being said and make a firm decision that from now on, you will see this matter the way God sees it instead of the way you've always looked at it.

To do that, you'll have to do the second thing God told Ahaz to do. You'll have to be quiet. You'll have to shut up all the mental jabbering you've been doing, stop thinking about your own opinions and listen—really listen—to what The Word says.

Do you realize it's possible to read great quantities of scripture and never really hear what God is saying in it? It's not only possible, people do it all the time. Here's how it happens. We'll read a verse or two and something in them will trigger another train of thought. We may start thinking about what Aunt Sally said about that scripture. Or what Grandma used to say. Or we may even let our mind wander off on something else altogether—all the while we're still reading our Bible! We end up with only a vague idea of what we read because we weren't really paying attention to The Word, we were paying attention to our own thoughts.

Reading The Word of God that way is like shooting scattershot at a flock of birds—you don't ever hit anything. To hear the voice of God through His Word, you have to take aim and zero in on every word as you read it. Instead of just breezing through the Bible reading it like you'd read a novel or a history book, read it deliberately.

Meditate on it by asking yourself, *What does that mean to me? How does it change my life?* Ask the Lord to reveal specifically what He is saying through that Word to you.

Read every verse with the attitude that *this is God speaking to me and I am going to do what He tells me to do.* Make a quality decision you're going to act on that word as quickly as you would the word of your doctor, lawyer or a very close, trusted friend.

Determine in advance that you're not going to bend The Word to fit your lifestyle. On the contrary, you're going to bend your lifestyle to fit that Word. With that attitude, your spiritual ears will be open to hear whatever God has to say.

Fear Not!

"But, Brother Copeland, I'm afraid I'll do those things and I still won't be able to hear the voice of God."

Well, stop being afraid of that! *Fear not!*

Instead take a step of faith and believe what Jesus said. He said you're His sheep and you hear His voice. So stop doubting Him and calling Him a liar. Don't ever, ever, EVER again say, "I can't hear God's voice."

Start agreeing with Jesus. Start believing and agreeing with The Word. Say, "The Word says I can hear God's voice and I believe it! I do hear the voice of God!"

Then put your faith into action. Open the ears of your heart and start listening for the voice of the Spirit, especially when you're reading The Word. Pay attention not just to the activity in your brain but to the quickenings in your inner man (primarily the area just below your chin, or chest area).

If you're not sure where to locate those stirrings, just think back to a time when you had what we sometimes call a "hunch." Suddenly something just dawned on you and you knew or understood something you hadn't known before. Those kinds of dawnings come from your bornagain spirit.

Purpose to become more aware of the promptings that arise from your spirit because they are the leading of God. Learn to trust them. The Holy Spirit will help you step out on them a little at a time.

Initially He won't be giving you risky, world-shaking kinds of leadings. When you're first learning to identify God's voice, it will be mostly yes and no answers, not to go sell everything you own and invest it in some off-the-wall business venture. He'll begin by showing you simple truths from The Word that you can act on. He'll reveal from The Word, for example, how you can obey more fully the law of love. He'll show you ways to bless the people around you.

The more you trust His voice and follow His leadings, the more clearly you'll find you can hear from Him. Before long, hearing from God won't be an occasional event but an every-day part of life. And when someone asks you, "What is the Spirit of God telling you today?" you won't hesitate a moment.

You'll know exactly what to say.

Prayer for Salvation and Baptism in the Holy Spirit

Heavenly Father, I come to You in the Name of Jesus. Your Word says, "Whosoever shall call on the name of the Lord shall be saved" (Acts 2:21). I am calling on You. I pray and ask Jesus to come into my heart and be Lord over my life according to Romans 10:9-10: "If thou shalt confess with thy mouth the Lord Jesus, and shalt believe in thine heart that God hath raised him from the dead, thou shalt be saved. For with the heart man believeth unto righteousness; and with the mouth confession is made unto salvation." I do that now. I confess that Jesus is Lord, and I believe in my heart that God raised Him from the dead.

I am now reborn! I am a Christian—a child of Almighty God! I am saved! You also said in Your Word, "If ye then, being evil, know how to give good gifts unto your children: HOW MUCH MORE shall your heavenly Father give the Holy Spirit to them that ask him?" (Luke 11:13). I'm also asking You to fill me with the Holy Spirit. Holy Spirit, rise up within me as I praise God. I fully expect to speak with other tongues as You give me the utterance (Acts 2:4). In Jesus' Name. Amen!

Begin to praise God for filling you with the Holy Spirit. Speak those words and syllables you receive—not in your own language, but the language given to you by the Holy Spirit. You have to use your own voice. God will not force you to speak. Don't be concerned with how it sounds. It is a heavenly language!

Continue with the blessing God has given you and pray in the spirit every day.

You are a born-again, Spirit-filled believer. You'll never be the same!

Find a good church that boldly preaches God's Word and obeys it. Become part of a church family who will love and care for you as you love and care for them.

We need to be connected to each other. It increases our strength in God. It's God's plan for us.

Make it a habit to watch the *Believer's Voice of Victory* television broadcast and become a doer of the Word, who is blessed in his doing (James 1:22-25).

About the Author

Kenneth Copeland is co-founder and president of Kenneth Copeland Ministries in Fort Worth, Texas, and best-selling author of books that include *How to Discipline Your Flesh* and *Honor—Walking in Honesty, Truth and Integrity*.

Since 1967, Kenneth has been a minister of the gospel of Christ and teacher of God's Word. He is also the artist on award-winning albums such as his Grammy-nominated *Only the Redeemed, In His Presence, He Is Jehovah, Just a Closer Walk* and his most recently released *Big Band Gospel* album. He also co-stars as the character Wichita Slim in the children's adventure videos *The Gunslinger, Covenant Rider* and the movie *The Treasure of Eagle Mountain,* and as Daniel Lyon in the *Commander Kellie and the Superkids*™ videos *Armor of Light* and *Judgment: The Trial of Commander Kellie.*

With the help of offices and staff in the United States, Canada, England, Australia, South Africa, Ukraine and Singapore, Kenneth is fulfilling his vision to boldly preach the uncompromised Word of God from the top of this world, to the bottom, and all the way around. His ministry reaches millions of people worldwide through daily and Sunday TV broadcasts, magazines, teaching audios and videos, conventions and campaigns, and the World Wide Web.

Learn more about Kenneth Copeland Ministries by visiting our website at kcm.org

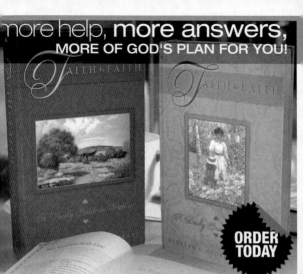

more help, **more answers,**
MORE OF GOD'S PLAN FOR YOU!

ORDER TODAY

From Faith to Faith (book) male-210004, female-210005 Best-selling daily devotional that delivers the faith-building teachings of Kenneth and Gloria Copeland in power-packed daily doses.

Kenneth Copeland Reference Bible 210001, 210002 Leather-bound study Bible containing Kenneth Copeland's personal study notes on prosperity, grace, righteousness, honor, faith, covenant and more.

To Know Him (paperback book) 301500 Living contact is not only possible...it's something He desires! Go beyond religion and enter into the most rewarding and fulfilling relationship you can ever have.

World Offices
Kenneth Copeland Ministries

For more information about KCM and our products,
please write to the office nearest you:

Kenneth Copeland Ministries
Fort Worth, TX 76192-0001

Kenneth Copeland
Locked Bag 2600
Mansfield Delivery Centre
QUEENSLAND 4122
AUSTRALIA

Kenneth Copeland
Private Bag X 909
FONTAINEBLEAU
2032
REPUBLIC OF SOUTH AFRICA

Kenneth Copeland Ministries
Post Office Box 84
L'VIV 79000
UKRAINE

Kenneth Copeland
Post Office Box 15
BATH
BA1 3XN
U.K.

Kenneth Copeland
PO Box 3111 STN LCD 1
Langley BC V3A 4R3
CANADA

**Kenneth Copeland Ministries
Singapore Ltd.**
My SingPost Box 880178
Singapore 919191

We're Here for You!

Join Kenneth and Gloria Copeland and the *Believer's Voice of Victory* broadcasts Monday through Friday and on Sunday each week, and learn how faith in God's Word can take your life from ordinary to extraordinary.

You can catch the *Believer's Voice of Victory* broadcast on your local, cable or satellite channels.* And it's also available 24 hours a day by webcast at BVOV.TV.

Enjoy inspired teaching and encouragement from Kenneth and Gloria Copeland and guest ministers each month in the *Believer's Voice of Victory* magazine. Also included are real-life testimonies of God's miraculous power and divine intervention in the lives of people just like you!

To receive a FREE subscription to
Believer's Voice of Victory, write to:
Kenneth Copeland Ministries
Fort Worth, TX 76192-0001
Or call: 800-600-7395
Or visit: **www.kcm.org**

If you are writing from outside the U.S., please contact the KCM office nearest you. Addresses for all Kenneth Copeland Ministries offices are listed on the previous page.

* Check your local listings for times and stations in your area.